Introduction

Greetings readers, thank you for purchasing my book! Before we delve into these delicious recipes I would like to provide you with some helpful information about the avocado fruit!

Avocados are in a league of their own! The majority of fruits are made up of carbohydrates while avocados are made up of healthy fats. Several scientific studies have confirmed the many health benefits associated with this tasty fruit, here are some of them:

Full of Nutrients

The USDA National Nutrient Database states that one 40 gram avocado contains the following:

- 64 calories
- 6 grams of fat
- 3.4 grams of carbohydrates
- Under one gram of sugar
- 3 grams of fiber

Avocados contain several vitamins including: C, E, K and B-6. They are also high in:

- Omega-3 fatty acids
- Beta-carotene
- Lutein
- Potassium
- Magnesium
- Pantothenic acid
- Folate
- Niacin
- Riboflavin

Despite the fact that the majority of calories in avocados come from fat they are fats that you should run to and not run away from! Avocados are high in beneficial, healthy fats that help to keep you satiated and full. When you eat healthy fats, they send a signal to the brain to switch off your appetite. Eating beneficial fats slows down the carbohydrate breakdown process which helps keep your blood sugar levels stable.

Healthy fats are good for the skin, they assist in boosting the immune system and they speed up the absorption process of fat soluble minerals, vitamins and other nutrients.

Heart Health

Beta-sitosterol is a natural plant sterol and avocados contain 25 milligrams per ounce. Beta-sitosterol helps the body to maintain healthy levels of cholesterol.

Healthy Vision

Avocados contain zeaxanthin and luetin; they are two phytochemicals that protect the eyes against damage from ultraviolet light. As mentioned earlier, avocados absorb fat-soluble antioxidants such as beta-carotene which can help to reduce age-related macular degeneration.

Prevents Osteoporosis

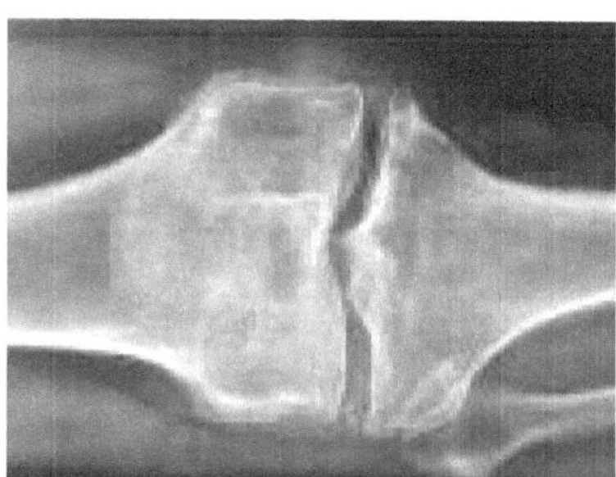

One avocado provides up to 50 percent of your daily recommended intake of vitamin K. Vitamin K supports bone health by increasing the amount of calcium absorbed by the body.

These are just a few of the health benefits associated with eating avocados, so I hope I have convinced you to eat them on a regular basis! Now the fun begins……. here are 30 delicious avocado recipes!

Bon Appetite………………

Avocado Smoothie Recipes

1: Strawberry & Avocado Smoothie

This creamy, delicious mixture is low in calories but high in fiber.

Preparation time: 5 min

Serves: 2 servings **Ingredients**

- ½ an avocado, peeled, pitted and sliced into chunks
- 150g strawberries cut in halves
-
- 4 tablespoons natural low-fat yogurt
-
- 200ml semi-skimmed Milk

1 1/2 cups ice

Lemon juice
Honey

Directions

1.   Blend all ingredients in a food processor until smooth.
2.   Serve in glasses.2: Tropical Peach and Avocado Smoothie

Smoothie made with avocado and juicy peaches.

Preparation time: 5 minutes

Serves: 2 servings **Ingredients**

- 2 cups of peaches, sliced
- 1 banana
- ½ an avocado
- 1 cup of ice
- 1 1/2 cups orange juice

Directions

1. Blend all ingredients in a food processor until smooth.
2. Serve in glasses.3: Spinach, Blueberry and Avocado Smoothie

Combination of blueberry, avocado and spinach that is mouthwatering

Preparation time: 5 minutes

Serves: 2 servings **Ingredients**

- 2 cups of orange juice
- 2 cups of spinach
- 1 cup frozen or fresh blueberries
-
- 1 banana
- 1 cup of ice
  ½ an avocado

Directions

1. Blend all ingredients in a food processor until smooth.
2. Serve in glasses.4: Avocado Chocolate Smoothie

Everyone loves chocolate.....combined with avocado this makes the perfect dreamy combination! Preparation Time: 5 minutes

Serves: 2 servings **Ingredients**

- 1 ½ bananas
- Half a large avocado peeled, pitted, and cut into pieces
-
- 21 teaspoon raw cacao powder3/4 cup soy milk or vanilla milk
-
-
  1 cup of ice
  A pinch of salt

Directions

1. Blend all ingredients in a food processor until smooth.
2. Serve in glasses.5: Avocado and Blueberry Smoothie

Delicious and healthy!

Preparation time: 5 minutes

Serves: 2 servings

Ingredients

- 1 cup of ice
- 1 cup orange juice
-
- 1 cup Greek yogurt, nonfat
-
-
  3/4 cup fresh or frozen blueberries

  Half a banana peeled and cut into pieces

1 avocado, peeled and pitted. Cut into pieces

Directions

1. Blend all ingredients in a food processor until smooth.
2. Serve in glasses.6: Berry-Cado Avocado Smoothie

This delicious combination of berries, avocados and kiwi

takes just 5 minutes to prepare

Serves: 2 servings **Ingredients**

- 1 ¼ cups of orange juice
- Half an avocado, peeled and pitted.
-
- 3/4 cup fresh or frozen berries
-
-
- 1/2 cup fresh or frozen strawberries

1 peeled kiwi
1/2 cup ice

Half a banana peeled and chopped into pieces

Directions

1. Blend all ingredients in a food processor until smooth.
2. Serve in glasses.7: Avocado and Cucumber Smoothie

Cool, smooth and easy to enjoy any time of day!

Preparation time: 5 minutes

Serves: 2 servings **Ingredients**

- ½ a long cucumber, cut into cubes
- Half a large avocado peeled, pitted, and cut into pieces
-
- 1/2 cup whole-milk yogurt
-
- 1 tablespoon chia seeds

1 tablespoon of honey
1 cup of ice

Directions

1. Blend all ingredients in a food processor until smooth.
2. Serve in glasses.8: Goblin Green Halloween Treat

This delicious combination of fruits and veggies makes for a wonderful Halloween treat!

Preparation time: 5 minutes

Serves: 2 servings **Ingredients**

- 1 ½ bananas, peeled and sliced into chunks
- 1/2 cup vanilla or soymilk
-
- 1/2 cup non-dairy milk, vanilla flavor
-
-
- 1 teaspoon matcha green tea powder
-
-
  3/4 cup watermelon or peaches

  1/4 avocado peeled, pitted, and cut into pieces

  Fresh spinach - A few handfuls

  1 cup of ice

Directions

1. Blend all ingredients in a food processor until smooth.
2. Serve in glasses.9: Avocado Acai Smoothie

Smoothie made with avocado, berries, and acai

Preparation time: 5 minutes

Serves: 2 servings **Ingredients**

- 1 ½ cups of soy vanilla milk
- 1 1/2 bananas, peeled & chopped
-
- 1 cup frozen or fresh blueberries
-
- 1 cup frozen or fresh strawberries

  1 cup acai juice

  1 cup of ice

Directions

1. Blend all ingredients in a food processor until smooth.
2. Serve in glasses.10: Avocado Combo Smoothie

Beautiful combination of avocado, celery and ginger.

Preparation time: 5 minutes

Serves: 2 servings **Ingredients**

- 1 ½ cups of coconut milk
- 1 avocado, peeled and pitted. Cut into pieces
-
- 1 banana, peeled.
-
-
- 1 medium apple, cut into small pieces
-

1 stalk celery, cut into pieces

One inch of ginger, peeled.

1 cup of ice

Directions

1. Blend all ingredients in a food processor until smooth.
2. Serve in glasses.Avocado Sandwich Recipes

11: Turkey Bacon, Hummus and Avocado Sandwich

Preparation time: 10 minutes

Serves: 4 servings **Ingredients**

- 1 ripe avocado, peeled, pitted, and cut into slices
- 8 slices whole grain bread
-
- 1/2 cup hummus
-

  8 strips of bacon-cooked turkey

  1 tomato cut into slices

Directions

1. Spread the hummus on all bread slices.
2. Layer four slices of bread with 2 slices each of avocado, 2 strips bacon, and 2 slices each of tomato.
3. Add the remaining bread slices.12: Apple, Feta and Avocado Sandwich

Avocado cream, crunchy apple, and creamy feta all in one sandwich
Preparation Time: 10 minutes

Serves: 4 servings **Ingredients**

- 1 ripe avocado, peeled, pitted and cut into slices
- 2 tablespoons of lime juice
- 2 tablespoons olive oil
-
-
- 1 tablespoon fresh mint chopped
-
-
- 1/2 cup baby arugula
-
-

1 apple, cored and sliced

14 English cucumber, sliced and peeled

6 slices of feta cheese

8 slices whole wheat bread

Directions

1. In a medium bowl, combine the oil, salt, mint, oil, and lime juice.
2. Place the avocado on four slices of bread.
3. Add feta cheese, cucumber, and apple to the top.
4. Serve with the remaining bread.
5. Cut into triangles and serve.13: Chickpea, Avocado Sandwich

Delicious combination of chickpeas and onions, as well as celery, celery, onions, and avocados!

Preparation time: 10 minutes

Serves: 4 servings **Ingredients**

- 1 can of chickpeas rinsed and drained
- 1/3 cup diced celery
-
- 1/3 cup medium onions, diced
-
-
- Half an avocado, peeled and pitted.
-
-
- Half a lime's juice

1 teaspoon kosher salt

Black pepper
1 sliced tomato
8 slices whole grain bread

Directions

1. Combine the onion, celery, and chickpeas in a small bowl and mash with a potato masher.
2. Mix in the avocado and lime juice. Season with salt, pepper, and cumin. Continue to mashing.
3. Spread the mixture on 4 slices of bread.
4. Top with the tomatoes.
5. Serve with the remaining bread. Cut into triangles and top with the rest.14: Egg Salad with Avocado Sandwich

Delicious sandwich made with spicy Dijon Mustard and creamy avocado!

Preparation time: 10 minutes

Serves: 4 servings **Ingredients**

- 1 avocado, peeled, pitted and sliced
- 6 hard boiled eggs
- 1 tablespoon white wine vinegar
-
- 1 teaspoon of Dijon mustard
- 1/2 teaspoon salt

  1/2 cup minced onion

  2 tablespoons of chopped chives

Directions

1. Peel the eggs and remove the yoke from two of them.
2. Take the rest of your eggs and chop them up.
3. Combine the eggs, avocados, onions, mustard, vinegar, salt and sugar in a small bowl. Mix all ingredients.

4. Spread the mixture on 4 slices of bread.

5. Cover the remaining bread with it, and then cut into triangles.15: Ploughman Avocado Sandwich

This sandwich is an improved version of the Irish corned Beef Sandwich. It features a combination of mushrooms, avocado, honey mustard and other delicious ingredients.

Preparation time: 15 minutes

Serves: 1 serving **Ingredients**

- 3 slices of thick rustic bread
- 2 ounces honey mustard
-
-
  1 ounce finely chopped chives
-
-
  5 ounces sliced corned meat
-
-

  1 avocado ripe, peeled and pitted.

  4 slices of Irish cheddar cheese

1 large Portobello mushroom, sliced, and roasted

1 sliced medium tomato

Directions

1. Preheat the oven to 200°C.
2. Spread honey mustard on three bread slices and sprinkle with chives.
3. Layer with avocado, cheese, and corned beef.
4. Layer the mushroom, tomato, and cheese on the other slice.
5. Bake the sandwich for 2 minutes.
6. After the sandwich has been baked, take it out of the oven. Place the third slice of bread on top. Top with the other half of the sandwich. Cut into triangles and enjoy.16: Avocado Hass Halftime Sandwich

This fancy party sandwich is made with feta, avocado, peppers, and grilled chicken.

Preparation time: 10 minutes

Serves: 4 servings **Ingredients**

- 1 tablespoon of olive oil
- 1/4 cup lemon juice
-
- 1/2 cup chopped dill
-
-
- Salt and black pepper
- 1 breast of skinless, boneless grilled chicken breast
-
- 1/4 cup diced cucumber
-
- 1/8 cup red onion finely chopped
-

1/4 cup diced tomato

1/4 cup diced red pepper

1 avocado ripe, peeled and pitted.

1/8 cup low-fat feta cheese, chopped

1 cup of baby spinach

2 Slices of whole wheat pitas cut in two**Directions**

1. Mix all ingredients in a medium-sized bowl.
2. Place the mixture in the pitta halves, and then serve.17: Veggie and Avocado Sandwich

Enjoy a fun, fresh way to enjoy your vegetables in a tasty sandwich with avocado.

preparation time: 5 minutes

Serves: 1 serving **Ingredients**

- 1 whole wheat pitta round
- 2Avocado ripe, peeled and pitted.A tablespoon of baby mushrooms
- slicedA few tablespoons of grilled artichoke heart1 red bell pepper,
- chopped
-
-
- 1/2 cup sundried tomatoes
-
-

1 teaspoon dried rosemary

1/2 teaspoon olive oil

Directions

1. Cut the pitta bread in half.
2. Place the avocado in the bread.

3. Layer the ingredients together and serve.18: Turkey, Brie and Avocado Panini

Hot melted brie and hot cool avocado are paired with slices of turkey.

Preparation time: 15 minutes

Serves: 4 servings Ingredients

- ½ a cup of olive oil
- 3 tablespoons balsamic vinegar
-
- 1 large clove minced garlic
-
-
- Salt and pepper
- 8 ounces thinly sliced turkey

10 ounces sliced brie

2 ripe avocados, peeled and pitted. Cut into 12 pieces.
One 16-ounce ciabatta bread

Directions

1. Pre-heat the grill to 200°C.
2. Combine the olive oil, garlic, vinegar and salt in a small bowl. Combine all ingredients thoroughly.
3. Spread the avocado, cheese, and turkey on the bread and then drizzle the dressing over it.
4. Add the rest of the bread to the top and then cut into triangles.
5. Grill for three minutes, then serve.19: Grilled Avocado, Chicken and Rosemary Sandwich

This sandwich is easy to make, but delicious!

Preparation time: 20 minutes

Serves: 8 servings **Ingredients**

- 4 boneless chicken breasts
- 12 ounces Italian dressing
-
- 3 tablespoons fresh rosemary
-
-
- 1 loaf of ciabatta bread
- Olive oil
- 2 Avocados   ripe,   pitted,   and   sliced2
  medium-sized ripe tomatoes, sliced Fresh
  ground chili

Directions

1. Pre-heat the grill to 200°C.
2. Mix the dressing and rosemary in a small bowl. Whisk together thoroughly.
3. Marinate the chicken for at least 15 minutes.
4. Grill the chicken on both sides for about 5 minutes.
5. Cut the bread into eight pieces.
6. Place the bread on the grill and brush with olive oil.
7. Serve the bread with the remaining sandwich filling.20: Avocado and Turkey Sandwich Wedges

This amazing combination of cheese, turkey, tomatoes, and avocado is simply incredible!

Preparation time: 10 minutes

Serves: 8 servings **Ingredients**

- 3 loaves of sour bread dough
- 2 Avocados ripe, peeled and pitted.
- 3 tablespoons of salsa
- 3 strips of roasted red bell pepper
-
-
- 1 lb. thinly sliced smoked turkey
-
-

3 slices of red onions rings

1 1 ounce sliced pepper Jack cheese
2 romaine lettuce leaves

Directions

1. You can make a shell from the bottom of the bread by tearing the inside.

2.   Combine the salsa and avocado in a small bowl and mix well.
3.   Spread the avocado mixture onto the bread.
4.   Layer cheese, turkey, onions and slices of avocado on top.
5.   Add the remaining bread to the top. Slice into triangles and serve.Avocado Salad Recipes

21: Grilled Chicken and Avocado Salad

Grilled chicken with avocado, garlic, chives and lettuce is a delicious combination!

Preparation time: 10 min

Cooking time is 15 minutes

Serves: 4 servings **Ingredients**

- 2 skinless, boneless chicken breasts
- 3Extra virgin olive oil in tablespoonsKosher salt
- Ground black pepper
- 1/2 cup mayonnaise
-
-
- 2 cloves of grated garlic
- 1/4 cup diced red onions
-
-
- 3 tablespoons of minced chives
  1 Large iceberg lettuce heads sliced into four pieces
  2 avocados, peeled and pitted

Directions

1. Pre-heat the grill to 200°C.
2. Sprinkle 1 tablespoon olive oil on the chicken. Season with salt and pepper.
3. For 5 minutes, cook the chicken on each side.
4. After the chicken has been cooked, take it off the grill and mash it with an fork.
5. Add the red onion, garlic and chives to a medium-sized jar. Cover the jar with a lid and shake it well.
6. Serve the iceberg wedges with half of an avocado, shredded chicken on top, salad dressing, and garnish with chives.22: Avocado Salad in a Jar

A unique way of eating a tasty salad with a great mixture of fresh and healthy ingredients

Preparation time: 20 minutes

Cooking time: 10 minutes

Serves: 4 servings **Ingredients**

- 2 tablespoons of red wine vinegar
- 1 tablespoon of Dijon mustard
- 1 clove of minced garlic
- 1 teaspoon of Worcestershire sauce
- 1/3 cup of olive oil
- 1 tablespoon of olive oil
- Kosher salt
- Ground black pepper
- 1 cherry tomato, halved
- ½ a pound of skinless, boneless chicken breast
  ½ a teaspoon of garlic powder
- ½ a teaspoon of lemon pepper
- 4 hard boiled eggs cut into quarters
- 4 slices of bacon, cooked and crumbled
- 1 avocado, peeled, pitted and chopped
- 1 tablespoon of lemon juice
- ½ a cup of blue cheese, crumbled
- 2 large romaine lettuce heads, chopped
- 2 tablespoons of chopped chives
  4 mason jars

Directions

1. Make vinaigrette by whisking together the Worcestershire sauce,garlic, Dijon mustard and red wine vinegar in a medium sized bowl. Slowly add the olive oil whisking as you pour. Season with salt and pepper.
2. In a large frying pan, heat the remaining olive oil.
3. Season the chicken with salt, pepper and garlic powder.
4. Cook the chicken for 4 minutes on each side.
5. Once cooked, transfer the chicken onto a chopping board and slice intosmall chunks.
6. Put the avocado into a small bowl and add the lemon juice, toss to coat.
7. Pour 2 tablespoons of the dressing into each mason jar.

8. Layer the jar with the salad ingredients.
9. Seal tightly, the salad can be kept in the refrigerator for up to 4 days.
10. Before serving, shake the jar thoroughly to coat the salad in thedressing.

23: Guacamole Salad

There is nothing better than some good old healthy Mexican food…..you will love this salad! **Preparation time:** 10 minutes

Serves: 5 servings **Ingredients**

- ¼ cup of extra virgin olive oil
- The juice of 1 lime
- ¼ teaspoon of cumin
- Kosher salt
- Ground black pepper
- 1 pint of cherry tomatoes sliced in half
- ½ a cup of corn
- ½ a finely chopped medium red onion
- 1 minced jalapeño
- 2 ripe avocados, peeled, pitted and cut into chunks
  2 tablespoons of chopped cilantro

Directions

1. Make the dressing in your small bowl by whisking together the cumin,lime juice, olive oil and season with pepper and salt.
2. In a large bowl, combine the salad ingredients, add the dressing andtoss them to combine.

24: Breaded Cobb Chicken Salad

Everything you love about salad with an added twist of breaded chicken!

Preparation time: 15 minutes

Cooking time: 20 minutes

Serves: 4 servings **Ingredients**

- 1 pound of skinless, boneless chicken breasts
- 1 cup of bread crumbs
- 2 lightly beaten eggs
- 2 tablespoons of extra virgin olive oil
- 1 large head of romaine lettuce
- 2 cups of cherry tomatoes cut in half
- 1 cup of corn
- ½ a cup of crumbled blue cheese
- 1 avocado, peeled, pitted and diced
- ½ a pound of bacon, cooked and sliced into pieces
- Kosher salt
  Ground black pepper

- Ranch dressing

Directions

1. Preheat the oven to 200 degrees C.
2. Line a baking tray with parchment paper.
3. Place the chicken in a shallow bowl and season it with salt and pepper.
4. Whisk the eggs in a separate shallow bowl and put the bread crumbsinto another shallow bowl.
5. Dip the chicken into the eggs and then into the breadcrumbs.
6. Arrange the breaded chicken onto the baking tray.
7. In a large frying pan heat the olive oil over medium heat.
8. Cook the chicken for 4 minutes on both sides.
9. Place the chicken back onto the baking tray and bake for 10 minutes.
10. When the chicken is cooked remove the tray from the oven and allow itto cool down.
11. Transfer the chicken onto a plate and cut into chunks.
12. Arrange the lettuce onto serving plates, top with the chicken, bacon,avocados, blue cheese, corn, and tomatoes.
13. Season with salt and pepper, drizzle the ranch over the top and serve.

25: Avocado Salad with Cumin and Lime Vinaigrette

This creamy, cool, spicy avocado salad is a healthy and creative addition for lunch or dinner. **Preparation time:** 25 minutes

Serves: 8 servings **Ingredients**

- 1 tablespoon of cumin seeds
- ¼ cup of lime juice
- ¼ cup of fresh cilantro leaves, chopped
- ½ a cup of whole cilantro leaves
- 2 tablespoons of rice vinegar
- 1 tablespoon of honey
- Kosher salt
- Ground black pepper
- ¼ cup of olive oil
- ¼ cup of vegetable oil
- 4 cups of argula leaves
- 2 pounds of ripe tomatoes
- 4 large ripe avocados
- 1 large red onion
- 1 teaspoon of ground cumin

Directions

1. Heat a frying pan over medium heat and toast the cumin seeds forapproximately 5 minutes until they start to become flagrant. Once cooked take the frying pan off the heat and allow the cumin seeds to cool down.
2. Whisk together the toasted cumin seeds, honey, vinegar, and choppedcilantro leaves, ¼ teaspoon of black pepper and 1 teaspoon of salt in a medium sized bowl.
3. Arrange the arugula onto a serving plate and top with the red onions,avocados and tomatoes. Drizzle half of the vinaigrette over the top, sprinkle with the chopped cilantro leaves and serve with the remaining vinaigrette on the side.

26: Arugula, Avocado, Mango and Shrimp Salad

Avocado and seafood are the perfect combination for a delicious salad!

Preparation time: 4 minutes

Cooking time: 6 minutes

Serves: 4 servings **Ingredients**

- 1 pound of medium shrimp, deveined and peeled
- 1 tablespoon of vegetable oil
- 5 cups of arugula
- 1 sliced avocado
- 1 diced mango
- ½ a medium red onion
- ¼ cup of extra virgin olive oil
- The juice of 2 limes
- A pinch of sugar
- A pinch of cumin

Directions

1. In a large frying pan heat the oil over medium heat.
2. Cook the shrimp until they become opaque, this should takeapproximately 4 to 6 minutes.
3. Combine the onion, mango, avocado, shrimp, and arugula in a largesalad bowl.
4. In a small jar combine the cumin, sugar, lime juice and olive oil.Tightly screw a lid on the jar and shake thoroughly.
5. Arrange the salad onto plates and drizzle the dressing over the top andtoss to combine.

-
-
-
-
-
-

27: Salad Shrimp Stuffed Avocado

A delicious salad stuffed into an avocado topped with crumbled feta cheese!

Preparation time: 5 minutes

Cooking time: 7 minutes

Serves: 4 servings

Ingredients

- 2 pitted avocados
  2 tablespoons of extra virgin olive oil
  ½ a pound of raw deveined shrimp
  1 cup of cherry tomatoes sliced in half
  ½ a cup of corn

¼ cup of Greek yogurt
The juice of 1 lemon
- Kosher salt
- Ground black pepper
- Basil

Directions

1. Scoop out the flesh of the avocado but leave some around the edges. Chop the avocado into cubes and set it to one side.
2. Heat the olive oil in a frying pan over medium heat.
3. Cook the shrimp for 7 minutes, once cooked, allow the shrimp to cooldown and then chop them into small pieces.
4. In a large bowl combine the corn, tomatoes, shrimp, avocado, Greekyogurt, lemon juice and salt and pepper. Toss to combine.
5. Divide the salad into 4 avocado halves and sprinkle with basil.

28: Raspberry, Avocado and Chicken Salad

This isn't your normal salad; this rare burst of flavors is absolutely delicious! **Preparation time:** 10 minutes

Cooking time: 25 minutes

Serves: 4 servings **Ingredients**

- 2 tablespoons of fresh lemon juice
  2 tablespoons of low fat sour cream
  1 tablespoon of pure honey
  1 teaspoon of Dijon mustard
  Salt and pepper
  1 teaspoon of poppy seeds
  1 pound of boneless, skinless chicken breast halves

- 1 ½ teaspoons of olive oil
- 1 avocado
- 1 pound of raspberries
- 6 ounces of mixed greens
- ¼ cup of sliced toasted almonds

Directions

1. Preheat the grill to 200 degrees C.
2. Combine the mustard, honey, sour cream, lemon juice, 1/8 teaspoon ofsalt, 1/8 teaspoon of pepper and the poppy seeds. Stir to combine.
3. Season the chicken with salt and pepper.
4. Cut the avocado in half, remove the seed and rub oil into the cut side.
5. Grill the chicken for 10 minutes, and the avocado for 5 minutes.
6. In a large bowl combine the greens, raspberries and 1 tablespoon ofdressing. Toss to combine.
7. Divide the salad onto plates and top with the avocado, chicken,raspberries and almonds and serve.

29: Lemony Crab Salad and Avocado

Tasty crab salad stuffed into avocados!

Preparation time: 10 minutes

Serves: 4 servings Ingredients

- 5 ripe but firm avocados
- 1 tablespoon of grated lemon zest
- 5 tablespoons of fresh lemon juice
- 1 pound of crab meat
- ½ a cup of diced radish
- ¼ cup of light mayonnaise
- ½ a cup of fresh chopped basil

Directions

1. Slice 4 of the avocados in half. Chop one avocado into cubed pieces.
2. Drizzle the lemon juice over the avocados.
3. In a large bowl combine the lemon zest, diced avocado, basil,mayonnaise, radishes, crab meat, and the remaining lemon juice.
4. Stuff the salad mixture into the avocado halves and serve.

30: Chicken Caprese Avocado Salad

An easy and quick dinner for two, it is the perfect summer salad made in only 15 minutes.

Preparation time: 5 minutes

Cooking time: 10 minutes

Serves: 2 servings **Ingredients**

- 1 skinless, boneless chicken breast
- Salt and pepper
- ½ a cup of fresh mozzarella balls cut in half
- 1 ripe avocado, peeled, pitted and cut into cubes
- 6 ounces of mixed fresh salad
- ½ a cup of cherry tomatoes cut in half
- ¼ cup of fresh basil, chopped

Ingredients for The Balsamic Vinaigrette

- 1 clove of minced garlic
- 1 teaspoon of dry basil

- 1 tablespoon of Dijon mustard
- 1 tablespoon of lemon juice
- ¼ cup of balsamic vinegar
- 1/3 cup of olive oil Salt
- and pepper

Directions

1. Preheat the grill to 200 degrees C.
2. In a medium sized bowl combine the balsamic vinegar, lemon juice,Dijon mustard, basil, garlic and salt and pepper. Whisk together thoroughly until the oil and the vinegar are combined.
3. Season the chicken breast with salt and pepper and cook it on the grillfor 5 minutes on each side. Once cooked remove from the grill and slice into cubes.
4. Divide the salad in three small bowls and top with the grilled chicken,mozzarella balls, basil, cherry tomatoes, avocado and spring mix.
5. Drizzle the balsamic vinegar over the top and serve.